"By sharing her own jou beside the grieving pare the experience of child lo in the same way. This book is a welcome resource for grieving parents as well as those who love them."

-Jenny Albers, bereaved mother of Micah Albers

"From a nurse's perspective: *Still Fighting* has helped me to understand my patients who are dealing with loss. I have learned how to talk to them, interact with them, and love on them. From a general perspective: EVERYONE needs to read this book! You will understand your bereaved friends and you will feel more comfortable helping others!"

-Miranda Kemp, Labor and Delivery nurse

"*Still Fighting* feels like a warm, understanding hug from one loss mama to another. Sydney writes with grace and compassion. Entering into the mess of grief with us, she invites us to explore that pain, all the while clinging tight to the truths and freedom found in scripture. A beautiful, must-read for any family still in the trenches after loss."

-Liz Mannegren, author of "*Embrace: Clinging to Christ Through the Pain of Pregnancy Loss*" and bereaved mother of Landon Alarik Mannegren

"I tend to stuff my emotions, quickly quoting the words God says of me. Sydney Hatcher has helped me so much in my own healing; she says what I think but won't allow myself to feel or say."

-Nancy Collar, Respiratory therapist and bereaved mother of Bobby Collar

"Through personal stories, poetry, and challenging reflection, Sydney allows us to have a glimpse into how to best support our loved ones - to meet them exactly where they are and show them the love of Jesus in the midst of their pain and their joy."

-Pastor AJ & Michele McGraw

STILL
FIGHTING

Battles of a Bereaved Parent

Sydney N. Hatcher

STILL FIGHTING

Battles of a Bereaved Parent

INVICTUS MANEO PRESS

CENTREVILLE, VA

ISBN- 978-1-64826-453-5

Printed in the United States of America

Cover illustration: Frani Matthews

Forever missed. Forever loved.

In honor of my daughter,
Carmen Grace Hatcher
November 30th, 2017- July 19th, 2018

And the precious families of:

Keller Bartlett
Bobby Collar
Claire Elizabeth Aldrich
Evelyn Grace Sudlow
Baby Philpott
Sophia Grace
Jaxson Gerald
Isla James Racer
Liya Warren
Everly Jo Ostler
Valentina Espinoza- Zarate
Micah Albers
Landon Alarik Mannegren

Contents

INTRODUCTION

The flowers that once covered the mantle have long wilted.
The casserole dishes, once filled with comfort, have been returned.
The "Sincerest condolences" have made their final debut.

The war has ended.

Why can't I rest?
Why can't I leave the trenches?
Why can't anyone see that my wounds are still bleeding?

Why am I…

STILL FIGHTING

These are the

Battles of a Bereaved Parent.

IT DOESN'T KILL TO BE KIND

Did you know that when your child dies in the hospital there isn't a magical door that leads right to your bedroom where you can crawl under the covers and hide from the world?

It is the one detail that still haunts me to this day.

Carmen passed away in my arms and at some point it was decided that our "goodbyes" were sufficient enough to walk away. Forever. As we pealed back the door separating what felt like holy ground and brand new territory, I felt numb.

The lights hurt. The sun had the audacity to shine bright. And life, without apology, continued.

Our bodies led us to the hallway, the elevator, and then to the parking garage. As we turned the key in the ignition, the fuel indicator light turned on. Another delay where we would have to "pretend" to do life instead of crumble.

Nate somehow drove to the gas station, got out, and pumped the gas. It felt so cruel. I wondered if it were possible for our car to grow a sign that read, "Please do not talk to us. And if you do, please be kind. Our daughter just died. We do not know what to do now."

And in that instant I knew that I would never be able to see what another person was enduring.

From the hallway, to the elevator, to the garage, to the gas station, to our 34-minute drive home I prayed for the grace that would enable us to get to a place where we could break, and in the meantime, that it would be possible for every person we encountered to just be kind.

My prayers continued as the weeks passed and I took my first trip out of the house alone. That was followed by my first trip to the grocery store, doctor's office, and to a restaurant. Every place seemed unfamiliar in my new form—broken. I would continue praying that others would see my sign that read, "Please do not talk to me. And if you do, be kind. My daughter just died. I do not know what to do right now."

Every time I walk into the hospital I am extremely aware that someone else could be taking their first steps into the harsh world with a newly broken heart. As I browse the isles of the grocery store I think twice before making remarks about someone's family size or appearance. As I pump my gas I take a deep breath and pray for the invisible signs all around us that no one can see, but everyone has.

I have no idea what the person next to me is facing. The only thing I can do to help them is to **be kind."**

There are two groups of people who have chosen to read this book. The first group read the previous entry and thought, "I know exactly how you feel." And the second group read the same entry and thought, "Dear God, I can't imagine!" The good news is that this book is for both of you.

In fact, I honestly believe that this book is for everyone. On the most basic level you will learn to be challenged with a new perspective by reading it. At best, you will have a helpful companion on your grief journey and perhaps be better equipped to become that helpful companion for someone else.

The death of a child fractures the natural order of the world. No matter the amount of faith, positive vibes, or strength you possess, having your child precede you in death will leave you burdened with questions and threaten to leave you defeated.

Armed with kindness, love, and a better understanding of your new battles, this book will present you with artistry to validate your emotions, find your new mission, and create your song of freedom your heart is desperately fighting for.

Be Kind.

As we enter the pages of this book, kindness is a two-way street. As a bereaved mother I pray for others to extend kindness to me. However, through my loss I have the choice to acknowledge the new eyes I possess and share kindness with others, including myself.

Before we begin, I would like to pray for you.

I pray that you are kind to others, as our battles are often secrets we keep.
I pray that you are kind to yourself, as your mind revisits the battles you have withstood.
I pray that you give yourself and others grace upon grace as you put on the armor of love.
I pray that you not only learn to survive the loss you have been handed, but also gain peace, purpose, and freedom, forevermore.
Amen.

The Guts of Grief

Grief will find you. In the midst of your day, as you try to find your way, grief will tap you on the shoulder and force you to cancel your plans. Grief will distract you from your responsibilities, send your heart racing and wipe your mind of reality. Grief will never truly go away.

Terrifying, isn't it?

But what if the grief we think we know isn't correct?

Our culture has corrupted grief. We are told that there are steps to overcome it, a timeline for it to phase out, that it is a burden and closure must be found to be able to enjoy life again.

What if we understood that grief is not a monster, but an emotion that exists only in the presence of love?

What if grief was actually love in disguise?

What if those times when we are suddenly overwhelmed by anger and doubt, drowning in our own tears, uncontrollably shaking with sadness... when our breath is ripped from our lungs and we crumble at a well-intended word... when we awaken in the middle of the night, drenched in our own sweat, craving one last hug...

What if this was love?

How does this perspective change things for us? Could we learn to welcome the intense presence of these feelings as a sign our love is strong? Could we find comfort in our ability to want to extend such affection to our child?

11

Love will find you. In the midst of your day, as you try to find your way, love will tap you on the shoulder and force you to cancel your plans. Love will distract you from your responsibilities, send your heart racing and wipe your mind of reality. Love will never truly go away.

The shift is so profound, I sighed in relief as the words hit the page.

But how does it look in real life and not just in a book?

I thought back to one of the first times I left the house after Carmen's death. For one reason or another, I needed winter boots. I pushed my almost 3-year old daughter, Holland, through the automatic doors of Target ready to conquer my mundane mission. It was so bright, so red. I didn't know where to start.

I began walking left but slowly realized the shoe department was in the opposite direction. The internal apologies began. "Oh, sorry. Okay. Pardon me." I felt ridiculous turning around. How did I forget where I was going?

We found the shoes and suddenly I couldn't remember why I was in that isle. The voices began. "What is she doing? She doesn't need new boots, her daughter just died!"

I couldn't breathe! I started believing the words and instantly doubted my ability to ever make a decision again. As quickly as I could, we got back in the car. Poor Holland was confused as to why our journey was so short and unfinished at that. The tears began and I sank into the driver's seat, completely broken.

Grief.

How could this be love?

I have to be exceptionally vulnerable to explain that on that day, just as the others, I missed Carmen entirely. I thought about her every second and thinking about her was my top priority. Boots, or anything else, didn't matter to me.

Target was a place that I knew was full of mommies pushing carts overflowing with children. I had always wondered what it would be like to have both my girls in tow for an outing such as this one. Walking in without her was crushing yet another dream.

I am almost obsessed with people knowing about Carmen because I love her. And being in a place full of strangers who get to glance into my "cart of one" left me feeling fake. No one here would know my truth. I felt alone, ashamed, and unheard.

Anxiety, doubt, and fear are the guts that my grief hides behind to strike me the hardest.

Could I really allow myself to pull their mask off and see the love that was bursting within me?

Could I stop in that isle and smile, maybe as tears fell, and think, "Hi Carmen, sweetie, I so wish you were here right now! Mommy loves you every second and I am thinking about you!"

Our grief fuels us. Forever more, this intense feeling will be the deciding factor to how we react to every single situation. If this grief is, in fact, love in disguise, recognizing its power can be detrimental in how we begin to move forward. Above anger, fear, doubt. Above money, fame, and success; love is the leading agent of change. Love is the propelling force for all of our reasoning, goals, plans and undeniable set of truths.

Your heart may quite literally feel as if it were sliced in two. There is great love pouring out. Uncontrollably, at that. It is escaping at a rate you have never experienced until now. You can choose to bury that love, or nurture it and let it bloom. Should you choose to neglect it, thorns of anger will surely poke through the dry dirt.

But if you nurture this love, just imagine the harvest!

Does your grief hide behind sadness? What about fear or doubt? Does your grief use isolation as a mask to capture your love and guilt to steal your peace?

Could you learn to pray as you became overwhelmed?

Lord.
It hurts. Coming here hurts. I am trying so hard to do something normal but I just can't. I miss my baby and I want others to be aware that my cart is only half-full today but my heart holds two.
I need your help to move.
Tell me who YOU think I am, right now, so I don't have to listen to those voices.
Give me grace as I encounter others who will never know my whole story.
Amen.

Self Reflection

What is the strongest emotion tied to your grief right now?

What is your favorite memory you have of displaying love to your child?

If your child were with you right now, what would you like to tell her/him?

Internal Battles

"Holland looked me square in the eye and said, "Mommy, I don't want to die."

I didn't know what to say to reassure her that she wasn't. How could I peacefully explain death to a two-year-old? At night I laid awake with my hands on my pregnant stomach praying I would feel a kick and, for what seemed like forever, I felt nothing. I couldn't reassure myself that Mia was still alive within me.

Slowly everything tightens and the seconds pound on me forcing the decision whether to breathe or cry. I become perplexed because genuine happiness seems to be ripped from my hands without warning. I feel robbed and question whether or not the happiness was ever real. Once the fog sets in it's hard to see past the five seconds in front of me and her purpose disappears.

The tightness is the worst. If I am not careful, the room spins until I am only able to sleep. It isn't restful, though. It is a trap.

When the morning comes I am reminded of its strength, for my eyes are weak and my breathing is shallow.

I lay awake counting the lies it spoke and preparing for its next attack. For now I know it isn't if it will find me again, but when."

Terror Attacks

"I had a nightmare about Carmen's death where I decided to give her my own heart in a last attempt to save her. In my dream I was conscious during the surgery and I awoke feeling like my heart was actually gone; cold, alone, and barely able to breathe."

I wish I could say that those feelings only arose after a terrifying nightmare, but many days they are my constant reality.

The first time I acknowledged my panic attacks was when I was pregnant with our third daughter, Mia. It was right before Carmen's first heavenly birthday. In my experience, a panic attack feels as if I am touching death without dying. I am crippled by darkness that radiates within my flesh and bones. The darkness covers every thought and leaves me physically and mentally useless.

The winter following Carmen's death I pulled over in an empty parking lot with tears streaming down to write:

"It is very unlike me to mope around with a cloud above my head. But today the war is in full force. It's beautiful out, the sun is shining, and I am planning Holland's third birthday

party. Mia is dancing on the inside and I want to be dancing on the outside.

"Then it happens. It can be triggered by a song, a word, a memory, or a place that completely stifles my next move. It is an emotion so strong that I go right back to that day she left my arms forever. And that's ok."

I won't stay here. This cloud will leave. The twist in my lungs will be released and I will breathe again. The sun will continue to shine and I will look up and wonder what that little cutie is doing. And I will smile!"

"My joy comes from Him. My strength comes from Him. Never hidden, I will always find my joy."

I remember feeling better after having written out my feelings, but slowly that "better" learned to mock me and throw me into a hypocritical, overly-positive, and unrealistic version of myself.

The lies I told myself started with: "You have to be okay."

I allowed myself to go through the sadness as long as I promised myself to find the good. I would take the shortest route to giving glory and most days it was sufficient. Then come the days where I can't limit my grief to a quick parking lot cry. The days where the memories are too horrendous to push back and everything just seems to come…

…crashing…

…down.

I sat on the ground playing with the girls and out of nowhere a chill went down my spine. It was a hot summer day in mid-July and it started pouring. I gasped for air as I tried to stay calm for my girl's sake. Without looking at the time, I knew.

"One year ago, to the minute, a storm like this arrived. I was at the hospital with my mom as Carmen went down for her very last procedure. This surgery was different than her others, though. Before she was wheeled away, the doctor looked at me and said, 'You need to call your husband right now. He needs to come.' I swallowed my fears and blankly looked at the white walls as we walked back up to the main level. We went outside. I needed to breathe.

I sat on a bench outside of the hospital and for the first time there was stillness instead of bustle. The quietness was crushing.
I listened for God. He told me to prepare for the worst. He told me I would know what it would feel like to have no hope. And He told me it would be okay.

Carmen's surgery was brief. We knew what that meant. The rain picked up and whipped the high-rise windows. Darkness filled the room as Nate tried to make his way to the hospital. He arrived late, wet; we were already broken.

That evening was the longest of our lives. We tried everything. The doctors told us it was time. Carmen told us it was time. I needed to hear it from God. Nate and I closed the door to the world and prayed one last time.

I will never forget how God spoke to me that day. The reality I had clung to for months finally had an ending. In tears, I walked to the counter where my writing sat. Shaking, I picked up a pen and wrote the last two words God gave me: "God will bless you for your faithfulness... in heaven." Nate thanked God for being so clear. My shoulders sank into his. My work as Carmen's earthly mother had come to its end."

The Master of Grief commands, "Rewind and replay!"

"I cried and I squeezed my head in the shower and the water wasn't enough to relieve the pressure. Involuntarily, I crumbled and leaned into the memories that I typically force myself not to think of. I see my daughter, intestines out, already covered in scars from the surgeries she shouldn't have made it through.

She doesn't deserve this! I smell blood and bodily fluid; I feel sick beyond imagination, putting lavender under my nose to come close to my own child. There is stillness; lifeless air. There is an ounce of hope but I know the truth is coming and it won't bring healing. She is wheeled away only to return with less than she had before. I hold back my tears as my own mother screams. The conversation to follow was one no person should ever have to be part of. Still, I do not cry. I tell myself she can hear me. Who am I to cry when she is the one in agony? Who am I to cry now? I am the one still standing."

Over and over I play that day in my mind. Even when I don't mean to, when it's not a good time, or when I am so exhausted. That's when I hear the whisper: "You could have done more! Your body failed her and this is your punishment. You couldn't have taken care of her anyway. You killed her!"

During a panic attack, the most irrational part of my being becomes my official spokesperson.

Another huge obstacle for me (and it hurts my heart to admit this) is that I have at times almost enjoyed facing the horrible memories because they were memories of her. And if I had less of them, I feared I would have less of her.

How can we learn to think of our child's passing and hold some part of it with honor and dignity? How can we reflect on the worst day of our life and find something good?

Of course, I have no idea how you came to be a bereaved parent. I don't know what memories haunt you. I don't know what lies creep into your being when you are just trying to get up in the morning. I don't know what steals your rest.

I can only tell you that I am so sorry. I hate that you have to relive such horrendous moments in time. My sincere hope and prayer for you is that you can prepare to face these moments with purpose and peace.

Father God,

These images in my mind distract me at least and consume me at worst.

I trust you and your word but the pain is too much for me to bear.

I am weak. I cannot see past the next twenty-four hours and I need you to hold me.

I don't want to stay in this darkness. I need you to rescue me and show me there is fruit from this loss.

Amen

Facing the Enemy Head-on

Do you remember the part in the Bible where Jesus was a glorified hero? When His friends were plenty, and He easily drifted off to a peaceful and just afterworld? Remember when He escaped heartache and pain and humiliation because He was Jesus? Remember when God loved Him so much that He protected Him from everything and yet God's will was accomplished?
No? Me neither.

When I was at my lowest I pleaded to God, "Can't you just make this day a little easier? Couldn't this pregnancy be easy for once? Haven't I endured enough? Can I just live the rest of my life in ease?" And He quickly answered, "It wasn't easy for Jesus."

I've spent many nights after that thinking of Jesus's death, why He had to die in that manner, and why we have to die in the ways we do. I have come to many conclusions and if you ponder it you will come to your own. But for me, it's about compassion. It's about becoming helpers, servants, people who build relationships, people who can love.

How willingly Jesus endured death. He knew the incredible state He would be raised to. Never easy, but always worth it.

I thought about the brilliant, wonderful truth of the gospel, and I thought of the lies that I was listening to.

As a writer, I decided that I needed to give my internal lies a literal face. I needed to face my enemy head-on! I wrote the lies that I heard one by one, pen to paper. I gave myself permission to entertain the lie. I found going face to face with the words that play over in my head to be therapeutic. Once I could visualize them they didn't have as much power over me. I could look at them, dissect their flaws, and talk myself through their inaccuracies.

As much as I believe that the Lord can use my grieving heart for His glory, I had to learn to recognize God's voice above the noise.

When the lie surfaces that I didn't do enough to save my daughter; I find confidence in God's plan for our lives, which includes the exact minutes we are to be earth-side. When a lie corners me into believing my daughter's death is punishment for my sins I remind myself of Jesus Christ's perfect sacrifice that covers all my failures with His precious blood.

It may seem small, silly, and unhelpful, but with repetition and focus on God's word I have been able to shift my grief from an outward appearance of attempted happiness to a genuinely joyful expectation of blessings from our savior!

I still often reflect on her last day. But as I have been blessed to see the beauty Carmen left behind, I cling to the impact she created and I do my best each day to love the person she is inspiring me to be.

"The peace I felt was not my own. Maybe I didn't truly feel it, but I needed everyone else to.

A tug-of-war between spirits raged within me. In slow motion I told you it was okay to go. I needed it to be okay. I needed to be okay.

My skin... like needles. I heard whispers of your hair as I rubbed it. The only part of you I could touch. Amplified as if under a microscope. I felt our hearts break... together. The next battle we would fight apart for a length of time only God knew. But the victory would be ours. It would be okay. I would see you again. This moment had to be enough.

I hate the day we grabbed our weapons of love and peace and threw them at the heavy clouds that attempted to bury us with dust and dirt and ashes. We should have never had to hold those things!

Gentle and bold we walked to the end. Not seeing the next inch of space, I held my breath as you took your last. Astounded by my own heartbeat, I knew your new journey had begun. I knew you would be okay. I knew you had won.

I'm down here fighting, baby girl! That love and peace I still apply each morning, and several times during the day. I won't let those heavy clouds bury me!

The dust, dirt, and ashes... they cover me and the rain comes and, baby girl, it soaks me to my core, but I'm not drowning; I am growing!

In the ground, I am breaking with strength I never knew I had. Rising up are colors within me more beautiful than I've ever known. Radiating out and up, my eyes will never lose sight of the sun. Washed by the rain and drenched in His love. I grew because of you!"

Preparing for Battle

As much as we can allow ourselves space, time, and grace to grieve, there will always be days where we will break.

Battle of the Birthday

"As her first birthday progressed I spent more time counting the minutes going by not knowing what to do with them. I am a planner. I like to do meaningful work. And here I was counting the moments as my deceased daughter's first birthday passed.

My phone rang and it was the genetic counselor from the hospital that worked with Carmen. She called to give her birthday greetings to our family. I was so touched. We chatted about Carmen and then about the new baby on the way. I don't think either of us meant to have that conversation in that moment, but it just happened. I was reminded again that no matter the testing, this baby could still have genetic anomalies similar to Carmen. In all honesty, that part doesn't exactly frighten me. But the fear of the unknown and the fear of thinking I'm not strong enough to do it again, and the fear of losing another child again was too much in that moment.

After our conversation ended I went back to the main floor where I laid on the couch again, unsure of what to do with the minutes. My heart rate was elevated and I was weak. My mom and Nate knew I didn't know what to do so it was suggested that we cut and eat the birthday cake that I had made that morning.

And that's when I cracked.

I couldn't do it! I had been pacing around this cake. I had been so excited about celebrating her life and bringing joy into our home on this day. I had taken and posted pictures on social media of the beautiful cake we would enjoy. But in reality I couldn't do it.

I wasn't ready. I couldn't celebrate without her. What was I thinking? Why did I think this was a good idea?

I cried uncontrollably and began having difficulty breathing. I went in and out of having enough energy to speak and being completely still. I could tell my body was done. It was trying to conserve what was left, so being still was the only option.

Fear had taken over and it had won. It cast every good thing out. It stole my peace and my joy. Fear told me I made a mistake. It told me I couldn't carry this next pregnancy. Fear told me that no matter what, I will always be afraid.

The emptiness that creeps in after this kind of battle leaves me unsure of who I am. I have been here before. It's where I understand my beliefs, but I don't have the strength to fight for them. It is a place that feels like nothing is worth it. It is a place where I have no choice but to surrender."

Though I don't know how to make sure these episodes never occur I can share how I work through them.

First, I allow myself time to be a mess. I have learned to stop apologizing for my messy state and save my energy for more important matters.

Secondly, I pray. I let the Lord into my battle and admit that I am too weak to go one more moment feeling alone. It is normally the case that praying sets a rhythm to my chaos and allows my mind and body to realign. This practice invites truth to penetrate the lies that crowd my mind in my distraught state.

And finally, I have learned to trust that those around me can handle my thoughts and feelings. This is huge! Having people on whom you can count is the key difference between barely surviving and finding hope.

Perhaps you have lots of support or maybe, like many bereaved parents, your circle has dwindled down to the remaining pictures on the wall. Later I will explain how I rebuilt my army but for now I want to talk to the reader who desires to help someone through their internal battles.

HOW CAN I HELP SOMEONE THROUGH THEIR INTERNAL BATTLES?

Empathy over sympathy.
Every. Single. Time.

From one person to another, the fact is that no one feels better or validated when someone says:
- "You are so strong! I don't know how you do it."
- "I could never do what you do!"
- "God wouldn't give it to you if you couldn't handle it."

We don't need a pep talk! Trust me; we don't know how we have put one foot in front of the other most days and being strong was never what we aspired to be. And if God likes seeing me cry myself to sleep every night then I guess you're right.

"At least you know you can get pregnant."
"At least you got to hold her."
"At least you have another child."
"At least..."

We know. Yes, all of that is true but right now our heart longs for one thing that "at least" will never fill.

If you ever get the unique opportunity to comfort someone who is crumbling with grief, please know they are not expecting you to reach up and pull their loved one out of a top hat.

They did not confide in you or peal back their fake smile for a vulnerable moment so that you can patch it back up with badges of experience. They are not relying on you to fix anything or make their situation better. Do not take on that impossible task.

But they *do* hope that for even just a moment they do not have to be completely alone in the storm. They wish someone could open their door and walk out of their comfort into the rain and say, *"Wow, you are completely drenched, my dear! I am so, so sorry you have to walk in the rain. Can I walk with you so you don't have to be alone?"*

Be there. As uncomfortable as it feels, just be there and don't try to offer a solution. In fact, being there is part of the solution. Acknowledge their loss as exactly what it is and do not try to rush the silver lining. You might think it helpful to offering either of the following:
"Hey, sweetie! I am so sorry you're drenched! I hear this weekend is going to be beautiful!" or *"Oh goodness! That looks miserable, here's an umbrella! See you soon."*

In either case the thought is that our pain is only temporary, and perhaps even unnecessary, and that it can somehow be fixed if only we try hard enough or were more grateful.

Step out of your car, your house, or your comfort zone and feel the drops hit your face. Let it soak into your shoes and become our companion as we figure out how to get to dry land today.

.

"When Carmen turned two in heaven it was my second time celebrating her birthday.

A whole year had passed and I was, in a sense, ready. I had planned in advance for the wave that would come and try to knock me down. I was armed for the likely event that I would cave and succumb to despair. I didn't overwhelm myself with planning the perfect party. I understood it would always be missing the most important part, the birthday girl herself—my precious Carmen.

They said it would get easier with time.
They said I would learn to manage.
They said I wouldn't suffocate this time.

Or did they? Maybe that's just what I assumed that they would say, because they don't seem to understand that every day without her is another 24 hours I feel disconnected from the love I want so badly to shower her with.

I should not be surprised that her birthday feels like an empty pit of built-up affection that is thrown into the fire; like misguided desire to rejoice.

It's an awkward dance that is mixed with rushed breaths.
It didn't get easier.
I didn't manage well.
Suffocation was unavoidable.
Only because I love her.
Maybe they will forgive me."

Self Reflection

How would you honestly rate your mental health at this moment?

What day or event are you most anxious about? What are some things you would like to do to prepare for it?

What do you wish your family and friends knew about your inner battles?

A New Mission

New Battlegrounds

When a parent loses a child a rebirth occurs. Awareness to things that never before sparked our attention becomes priority. And life as we know it is made new.

"New" doesn't sound like a bad word, but I have never cringed harder than when I was informed that I would come to find my "new normal," or that God would give us "something new or something better" after Carmen's death.

What was wrong with our old way? I don't want to replace her!

It all seemed too cruel to digest.

But almost immediately I noticed that having a child in heaven altered my perspective. Right away I began to see sunsets with new eyes, hear songs with new ears, speak with new understanding, and live with a renewed sense of purpose. And, as much as I didn't want to admit it, there were some things that were… *better.*

"It was my first Mother's Day without Carmen and I lay in the same hospital where she passed. I was a patient in the high-risk unit on bed rest with Mia. (My girls like to come early) As you might imagine, it had all the parts and pieces to build a horrible day.

I was messaging with a dear friend about my urge to smash melons. (Stay with me here.)

It might be that it was day twelve of hospital bed rest, that the last two Mother's Days had been spent in this hospital, or it could have been that I felt smashed and wanted to see something that looked as bad as I felt.

Joking about this idea we imagined me with my hospital socks sneaking to a window and throwing watermelons to the pavement below. I thought about wanting to count how long it took to explode and if I would hold my breath as it fell. I thought about wanting to go down and see what was left and how far the debris reached. Above all, I wondered if the remains would be equally messy or equally beautiful.

When my world crashed and burned as the hopes and dreams I had for my daughter ended with death, I felt like a melon that had been smashed beyond repair.

I became messy, broken, and leaked all over things. My pieces were scattered further than I could imagine. I became a completely different substance.

I had tried to scrape those pieces off the ground and build what I thought a melon could look like again. I thought maybe in a few days, months, or years it would be possible for me to resemble that melon again. Maybe I would eventually stop making a mess.

But what if we aren't supposed to be melons? What if the smashing is the only way to become something new? And what if that mess we initially see is actually beautiful?

Today I am fruit juice. But isn't fruit juice awesome? It's sweet and delicious.

In my new state I can move more freely. I can be carried in a different manner. I am no longer held together by a skin that gets bruised. I am no longer pushed aside to pick one that's more perfect. Today I smile when I think of smashing melons. Smashing perspectives; smashing perfection. It's obliterating the desire to collect my seeds with sticky hands for absolutely no reason.

God is doing a new thing.
God is making ALL things new.
God is smashing us, not to end us, but to turn us into what we were always supposed to be."

...supposed to be.

What am I supposed to be?

That can be a tough question for someone who is just trying to figure out how to survive this next hour. But if you're willing, I pray you will entertain the idea that there truly IS purpose to the brokenness enveloping you.

Whether we want to accept the new life we have been handed is ultimately our choice. But for now, let's just spend time in gray space.

"The place I live now is mostly gray space.
There can be sorrow in my mind and a smile on my face.
I will laugh too loud when the world asks me to cry, but they
don't know every hour I turn to the sky.

I squint at the sun, half seeing her there.
I pray to God with thankfulness but wish He could share.

The grass dims as the clouds break.
I'm half-gone. It's not a mistake.
She is His and forever mine.
It's all gray, except the sunshine."

Most days I accept the new life I have been given with a grateful heart and tearful eyes. I think that's the best way I can explain what it is to be alive.

This world is broken. There is nothing here that can fill the void that heaven could surely provide.

But, I must move… here. Throughout my day, throughout my grief, I must keep moving.

Could this have really been God's perfect plan? Was this what was always supposed to happen?

Keep moving…

And what if while I am slowly moving I decide to believe that there is an astounding, necessary, and wonderfully beautiful reason that my daughter had to be taken from me?

"What if everything that makes me thankful
came from knowing her?
What if everything that makes me useful
came from loving her?
What if everything that makes me happy
came from losing her?
What if healing doesn't look like moving on but
pursuing a life completely shaped by the hole
she left?
What if my eyes, which long to see her face,
become overwhelmed by gratitude for her place
in heaven?
Then, my dear, am I restored?

And what if everything that makes me thankful
comes from knowing you, God?
And what if everything that makes me useful
comes from loving you, God?
And what if everything that makes me happy
came from losing myself?
What if healing doesn't look like moving on
alone but pursuing a life completely shaped by
the hole you fill?
What if my eyes, which long to see your face,
become overwhelmed by gratitude for my place
in heaven?
Then, oh Lord, have I felt your grace?"

May my prayer be an encouragement that gently challenges you.

Dear bereaved parent,
In this moment I plead that you know that your child was created perfectly by a Creator who loves him or her unconditionally.
I pray that you recognize that your beautiful child was given a mission on Earth that concluded prior to yours.
I pray that you can feel his/her hand upon you, wherever you go.
Although they do not walk amongst you, I pray that you choose to joyfully pursue the new purpose he or she has left you.
I pray that you have unwavering faith in the fact that your child is in the most magnificent place and that one day, when your mission is complete, you will reunite with them in paradise.
Amen.

Tiny Victories

"Holding her for the very last time, my life was altered forever.

I experienced letting go of every moment I ever had as well as those to come. That last day I experienced the courage to stand up after her heart stopped beating and smile after seeing a lifeless face. Fortitude to keep walking, knowing I'd never see her first steps, and the courage to continue living because I have to believe that my eternity is long and beautiful and worth all of this pain.

That last day was her first in paradise. It was the first time she didn't feel pain, struggle to breathe, and wasn't bound by tubes and lines. That last day she completed her earthly mission. She was a seven-month old servant of the Lord. That last day was so much more than the end.

It was the beginning: New love, new truth, and new life.

Because of her I want to celebrate beginnings. Without knowing the future, I want to celebrate blossoming ideas, early creations, and a brand new life. I want to celebrate tiny seeds, the sunset before it's in full color, the smell of a meal before I taste it. I want to celebrate the things to come. I want to learn to be thankful for the blessing before it arrives; never waiting for the last day."

Call to War

"All night I had dreams of the PICU. I saw murders and awful things. I saw the faces of the people who cared for my daughter and wanted to hug them so warmly. They were just dreams but they felt so real.

I thought again of Carmen's death and replayed every second of those five days leading up to her last breath. I thought of lying next to her again. And I thought, yet again, about leaving with empty arms.

The next morning my mom went to visit her friend who had brought us food when Carmen passed and this time she was returning the favor. Her friend's daughter was on life support just a few doors down from where Carmen died.

I knew that God prepared my family for this: death. It is difficult to admit, but death will surround us for all our days. I know God has called us specifically to care for the sick, the broken, and the families that tiny warriors leave behind.

My mom's friend expressed that when she knew it was time for her daughter to pass she remembered the picture of me and Carmen lying side by side in the hospital bed and she decided she wanted to do the same thing. She wanted to have one more sleep with her daughter before she would be gone.

The pride I felt was more than I would have thought hearing something like this. But to me it meant that even when Carmen was dying she was still impacting others by creating a way for loving moments to be cherished.

The prayers I have said for this mother today would have never entered my mind if I weren't well acquainted with this pain. But my heart is singing because I know how God can use death for good, for purpose, and for love."

Carmen

This is probably as good of a place as any to share a little about what Carmen's life was like.

Carmen Grace was born premature and taken to the NICU immediately. All three pounds of her were poked and prodded as specialists became curious of the "red flags" that began to surface. Our fresh newborn baby was suddenly deemed "rare" "genetically imbalanced" "sick" and "unknown."

Carmen lived in the Pediatric Intensive Care Unit for 194 days receiving countless procedures as she broke stigmas and statistics; proving over and over again that she was a fighter!

Being Carmen's mother was difficult. Her milestones were not typical and our life in the hospital was dark, sterile, and full of fear. But every single day Carmen kept fighting.

Without hesitation, she equipped me with helping hands and an unusual joy that proved to bring light and excitement to her home within hospital walls.

It started off small, as I placed tiny bows on her dark brown locks. It was the only normalcy I could give her beneath tubes and wires. Soon, it grew into weekly photo-shoots, make-shift outfits, decorations and themed props. Her hospital room became an art gallery and Carmen was surrounded by beauty. We began celebrating holidays and non-holidays alike. Even the horrible days, Carmen instilled in me a desire to create good moments myself and keep celebrating.

Science says that Carmen was not supposed to have been born. However, I argue that Carmen was not supposed to die. Not when she did and certainly not how she did.

You see, Carmen was thriving. Her life looked a bit different, but despite her disabilities, Carmen was doing well. So well, in fact, that she got to come home. Carmen got to experience family. She saw day and night and felt the summer sun on her skin. Carmen smiled and just days before death's grip took hold of her, Carmen laughed. It was the most beautiful belly laugh I have ever heard. To this day if I concentrate hard enough I can still here it.

Did God not see how hard she already fought? Did He not care what she had overcome? Was her purpose to endure such pain and suffering only to laugh once. Were her 232 days on earth truly sufficient?

Were her love lessons and sessions of suffering enough to penetrate my heart forever?

What about you? I don't know the amount of time that God gave your child to complete their mission. I do know however, that be it five minutes or twenty-five years, on this side of heaven it would never seem long enough.

Maybe it isn't the amount of life that matters so much as the amount of love shared.

Maybe my Carmen came to train me for celebratory combat. My voice is no longer timid, but bold to advocate for the weak and broken. Maybe her purpose was to propel me into the person God needed me to be. The compassion she gifted me could not have been formed had I not held death in my palms.

I am positive that your child has imprinted your heart with a new mission. A specific situation in your world needs to be improved and you have the power to redeem. Within your loss a magnificent truth has been revealed to you and your heart leaps at the thought of telling others.

God chose you! You have a mission! You have a purpose, and this pain is part of it.
Do not ignore the heart tugs; you have been prepared.

It will not be easy. It will not be comfortable. But your story is one of victory and beauty. You have something wonderful to offer the world that would have never been discovered if your child hadn't come into your life and then passed on to life eternal.

Dear Lord,
Thank you for the renewal of each day.
Thank you for holding the knowledge of our mysteries.
Thank you that each new sunrise allows us a chance to
try again.
I praise you for the mission that you have extended to us
so that we may compose our sorrow into glorious songs
that will alter existence.
Through the deepest pain you have chosen to mold us
into great and powerful pioneers of good.
Thank you.
Amen.

Self Reflection

How has losing your child changed your values and priorities?

What lesson(s) do you believe your child has taught you?

How will you strive to incorporate your new values and priorities into your daily life?

Life after Loss

Surprise Attacks

Ninety days after Carmen passed, my life looked strikingly different. Carmen had led me down a path to action; executing the lessons she taught me as her "medical mama."

My passion for helping others celebrate grew. I found myself inspiring parents to commemorate their children's unique milestones and equipping moms and dads with tools to bond with their children through bleak diagnoses.

In three short months I published her life story, *Carmen "The PICU Baby,"* founded the non- profit organization, Carmen's Miracle Makers, and discovered that I was expecting. Yes, the woman who wore her daughter's ashes in a pendant around her neck had life growing inside her.

I debated elaborating on our pregnancy after loss in this book because I feel that being blessed with another child was not the "happy ending" I perceive so many assumed it was after such a tragedy.

To an outsider, the chance at another pregnancy might seem to hasten the grief process or nullify it altogether, but there is absolutely no truth to that.

Mia has endured the grief journey not just with but within me. She is a gift and I will forever be overwhelmed that God decided the world needed her and appointed me to be Mia's mom. But never for one second was Mia's purpose to *replace* Carmen.

"Tulips. Oh, how I love you.

In 2015, the day after returning from The Netherlands, Nate and I found out we were expecting. After we got over the shock, we thought, 'Wow, he or she was with us in Holland.' To us Holland was one of the most beautiful places and God's presence was so evident! And that became her name—Holland.

A year and a half later as I watched our second daughter, Carmen, fight to survive in her NICU isolete, her diagnosis arrived. And with it a poem we read entitled, "Welcome to Holland." The story seemed to depict our life and those tulips became a symbol of God's hand over our daughter's life. Beautiful for those who choose to see.

Carmen's life was miraculous. The darkness seemed to press into her when all she tried to do was grow. When spring arrived, so did she. There was brightness and hope for the future as we finally could take our baby home.

But she was a tulip. Her season was short. Not less beautiful, not less anticipated, not less celebrated, not less breathtaking, and certainly not less colorful.

She came for such a time as she was appointed bringing joy to all who wanted to see.

As her petals fell and her stem wilted, darkness arrived again. The ground looked bare and it all seemed too fast. Winter took its inevitable place and yet her joy never left me.

I could not see the beauty that was coming. I could not see the bulbs below the ground. I did not know that one would grow again. I did not know spring could come again.

And then, just like a tulip, we found out about you, Mia. You are a living, breathing reminder that there is light after darkness. There is assurance that every winter has the courage to turn into spring and that God makes everything beautiful in its time."

Mia was a brand new human being, was part of our dreaded "new normal," and was different. In fact, everything was different.

In my pregnancy after loss:

- There was no "safe zone." We bypassed waiting those twelve key weeks to announce our pregnancy because we felt that was the right thing for us. We knew that we wanted to celebrate this baby and we knew that if this baby entered heaven before us we would need our support system to know of her.

- I had a sense of peace that even if I were to miscarry, this child would go to heaven to join his/her sister. And, oddly enough, that made me just as joyful.

- Telling my family was difficult. We were all freshly navigating our grief and everyone processed the news differently.

- My birth plan changed drastically and now I had a "death plan" in place.

- I worried constantly about my oldest daughter adjusting to this baby. I didn't want her to fear losing another sibling.

- This wasn't my "rainbow baby." I do not like how it implies that what came before was strictly storm. While Carmen's life was indeed beset with many storms she was so much more. Never could I view our time with her as pure darkness.

66

- I wanted to embrace this pregnancy more than my two previous. I wanted bump pictures and a shower. I wanted to look nice delivering her and have newborn pictures taken. I wanted our close-knit tribe to enjoy every moment of the journey heart-to-heart, shoulder-to-shoulder, soul-to-soul. I knew how quickly it goes and we never know what tomorrow brings.

- I did not pray for a healthy pregnancy. I had a new perspective on life and the value each person holds whether healthy or not. And so for me health was not front and center.

- I was so very happy and that was okay.

"We began going through Holland's and Carmen's belongings to see what items we still need for Mia. It seems impossible that time has passed to the point of having such a collection of tiny clothes.

I had a change of heart when opening Carmen's boxes that I had originally felt guilty for reusing. It was suddenly replaced by joy and honor.

There are specific things we agreed are strictly Carmen's but there were others I know are precious gifts left behind for her baby sister.

Holland joined in when she saw Carmen's things reappear and joyfully exclaimed, 'We have everything we need for Carmen!' I calmly explained, once again, that Carmen could not come back, so these things are gifts we can use for baby Mia. After a bit of anger in correcting names Holland looked up to the ceiling and said, 'Thank you, Carmen! Mia will jump out of Mommy's belly and open this box and say surprise!'"

Oh Lord, what wonderful surprises you have for us!

Father God,

The gift of a child is precious.

I pray now for all the wombs next to hearts that have endured death.

I pray that you would comfort and pour out confidence and joy upon the family expecting once again.

I thank you for their courage and desire to love once more.

Grant peace, Lord.

Peace that surpasses all understanding.

Amen.

Self Reflection

If you are expecting or hope to have another child in the future, what is your greatest fear?

What do you intend to tell your future children about their sibling in heaven?

What do/would you want your family and friends to understand about your current or future family dynamic?

Do Not Frighten
the Children

Holland was two and a half years old when her sister entered heaven. Many well intended people warned me of Holland's future after such a traumatic event. I spent days rehearsing my words to her, wanting Holland to remember her sister, simultaneously fearing my words would become daggers to her young ears, or worse, lies.

To the people who reassured me that Holland was "too young to remember any of this," I want you to know that you broke my heart.

To the people who spoke of nightmares and behavior issues, providing resources of counseling for Holland just days after Carmen's death, I wish you knew that I doubted my role as a mother because of you.

To the people who expressed that death is an uncomfortable conversation that should be avoided and replaced with words like "she's sleeping," I wish you understood how capable children are.

I wish you knew that Holland remembers things about Carmen that I can't rapidly recall. She knows her sister's name and says it whenever she desires. I wish you knew that the sound alone is music to my ears.

I wish you knew that Carmen's death has had enormous effect on Holland, so enormous that we are convinced she will work in the healthcare industry one day. She owns four stethoscopes, draws up her own allergy medication with accuracy, and preforms her own checkups at the doctor's office. The compassion and joy that flows from Holland is never-ending.

I wish you knew that Holland's questions about death sting me to my core. Sometimes they come from a place of fear and uncertainty. Other times her innocent proclamations steady my walk with the Lord, inspiring me to lead her in truth and love.

Above all, the death of Carmen led me to have conversations with Holland that I would have delayed for years to come. Holland expresses an anticipation of heaven that I have never known in any other form.

"Can Carmen come back down?"

"Does God give Carmen a bottle?"

"Will Carmen be here for Halloween?"

"I will just pull her down today and she will be SO happy!"

"I'm going to miss Mia when she goes to heaven."

"Don't worry Mommy, Carmen is happy. We will see her again."

"Mommy, you remind me of Carmen...because of your heart."

- Holland, age three

There are many variables to consider when navigating difficult conversations with your children. Their age, role and personality are all factors. As scary as it can be to hold this responsibility in your hands, please know that no one else could do a better job than you. Your children were entrusted to you and you know best!

In our circumstance, Holland was young but curious. She was accustomed to hospitals and thrived around people; young, old, and of all abilities. Shutting the door on Holland's interests could temporarily comfort me from my triggers, but may replace Holland's curiosity with fear.

I started simple with a truth that was as factual and as concise as I could make it. *"Carmen was too sick to live with us. God is taking care of her now."*

As time went on, and the question arose, I stayed the course. *"Carmen could not stay on Earth because she was very sick. God is caring for her perfectly and she is not in pain anymore."*

Whether or not you believe in God or Jesus or heaven, please understand; Children can sniff out a fake.

More than Santa, the tooth fairy and the Easter bunny combine, your child has come to you with a question that will impact their belief system. You need to be confident in your beliefs and speak assurance over them. Just as any other aspect in parenting, please vocalize your truth to your support system so that they can echo your values and set a firm foundation and instill confidence in your child.

Above all, children are not looking for you to have the perfect words eloquently ready to win an award. They are seeking warmth from your voice alone. They might be confused or scared or mad and they are looking to you for a secure embrace, even tearfully, with love and compassion.

"Look Mommy!!!! Look!!!! It's God coming down from the clouds!!!!" Holland exclaimed as we pulled into our parking spot.

I gazed up to the sky, half believing her. The clouds were moving fast and darkness was rolling in. Spots of brightness swallowed up the more somber colors as they knit together a beautiful work of art. But I didn't see God.

I turned around in my seat and softly said "One day He will come down Holland. Did you know that?"
She was undefeated and said "Yes mommy, and we will smile so big!!"

"Yes baby! That will be the best day ever."

"Dear God,
Thank you for healing us.
Thank you for the trees.
Thank you for living in our hearts and helping us
grow big, but not SO big- like you!
Thank you for taking care of Carmen for us
because she was too sick for Earth.
Amen."

-Holland, age 4

Self Reflection

What are the greatest fears or challenges you face with your other children since your family's loss?

What conversations would you like to have with your children about their brother or sister in heaven?

How do you see your children participating in their brother or sister's legacy? (This can be as simple as reading a special story in their honor or more independent such as raising money for a cause)

'Til Death Do Us Part

Marital Battles

I think it's essential that I touch on one of the greatest challenges bereaved parents face, which often takes the shape of tremendous pressure on the marriage relationship.

Most published models that rank life's stressors do not list the death of a child. Death of a spouse is ranked as the highest stressor, but many practicing mental health professionals with experience in family dynamics consider the death of a child as number one.

This is critical information because the tremendous amount of physical, emotional, and mental stress from losing a child can become wired into the very fabric of the most intimate of relationships and prove catastrophic. Divorce can be a real threat in such cases.

"For many months I didn't sleep. I would lay awake with my phone clenched in my hand awaiting the call that Carmen's health had declined yet again.

I would start my day with calls to her nurses and for hours I would pace around the house unsure of where to be.

I would try to parent my two-year-old, Holland, as I listened to doctors and social workers all afternoon. I was afraid to shower for the fear of missing an important call. I would sanitize the house in the hopes of avoiding any chance of us getting sick as even the common cold could mean the end for Carmen.

In the afternoon I would strategize who could watch Holland as I made my 45-minute drive to the hospital. I wore only what was comfortable. At the hospital I would assume the role of Carmen's nurse advocating for her life and trying to show her any ounce of love that I could.

One night after this routine, Carmen almost passed away in my care. I was exhausted. I felt alone, unseen, and angry with myself, God, and my husband Nate.

I was barely able to keep my eyes open as I drove home; I was beyond tired. I was hungry and I didn't know if Carmen would make it through the night.

It was around 1:00AM when I walked into our home and saw every toy sprawled out on the ground. The couch cushions were thrown in a pile and the blankets were askew. There was a half-eaten banana on the ground and the core of an apple beside it. By the stairs were Holland's dirty clothes and a dirty

*diaper. The kitchen had a pile of dirty dishes and an empty
pizza box on the counter. I peered into Nate's man cave and
saw him sound asleep.*

*In that moment the feeling of intense anger took hold of me
and I started shoving things around, making the initial mess
bigger. 'I'll show Nate that two can play this game!' I thought.
And I began internally listing of all the things I wanted to
scream at Nate and then wept.*

*I fell to the floor and said, 'God, I can't do this! This is too
hard. I can't save Carmen. I can't even be a good mom to
Holland. I can't save my marriage and tonight I don't even
want to! Maybe this would be easier if I were a single mom.
The husband you gave me isn't helping me at all. Look at this
mess! Why do I deserve this?'*

I sobbed and sobbed until God said:

'Sydney, put on my eyes. Your husband didn't sleep well last
night either. He got up and went to work so you don't have to.
All day he suppressed his emotions because he knows he can't
be at the hospital. He worries just as much as you. He wants to
talk but he doesn't know what to say.

On his way home he picked up a pizza because he knew you
were not able to make dinner. When he got home he was
exhausted but he knew Holland wanted to play. He made sure
to make her laugh in your absence. Those cushions and
blankets were a beautiful castle. There wasn't much food here,
but Nate knew you would want Holland to eat something
healthy so he fed her an apple and a banana. He changed her
diaper and put fresh pajamas on her before lovingly putting

her to bed. He walked downstairs and wasn't bothered by the mess because in his eyes he was thankful for being able to accomplish another successful night as a *single dad*. He thought about doing the dishes but his body ached and he fell asleep just as I asked him to. He needs to rest, because tomorrow he'll do it all again.'

Love isn't always beautiful or romantic or exciting or clean. Sometimes love doesn't look like love at all. But God is love, and when we put on God's eyes, we can see a love greater than this world can comprehend."

Putting on God's eyes has helped me countless times as Nate and I navigate this broken path of loss. There are days where I have so much anger built up and Nate becomes an easy target for my sadness to pin down. I have pleaded to God from the comfort of my damp pillow to give Nate some of the horrid images that keep me up at night. It usually takes hours for me to calm down and praise the Lord for allowing one of us to be free from torment. For the sake of our family to function on the most basic level I am grateful God has spared us each from one another's demons.

As a restless perfectionist, my seeking after mental health assistance came as a surprise to Nate—perhaps more of a shock, actually. I remember hanging up on him after his reaction to my diagnosis was less than empathetic.

Days later I gathered my pride and realized I had not been fair to Nate. By pretending to be more put together than I actually felt, I had misled him. I had completely discounted Nate's opinion and bypassed working on something together and instead sought after a quick fix for my misery. As much as I have to take full ownership of the desire to improve my mental health, there is nothing separate in a solid, fully functioning marriage. And what a gift it was that I could choose to lean on my husband through this battle as well!

I have heard it said that men and women cope differently. I would like to propose that every single person copes differently—different methods, different means, and at different times.

Grace, love, and mercy. Limitless amounts of relentless, unconditional love is the only thing that can supply strength to a couple stuck in the pit of loss.

Husbands and wives, it may temporarily feel good to distance yourself from one another, to escape your new reality, and to let the wrath of guilt swallow the love you share. I lovingly challenge you to hold tight. As in the reflection you see in the mirror, your marriage might look broken but with intention and care it can radiate beauty and strength. It can become a foundation so solid only GOLD will flow from it!

As the months and years pass, do not be surprised to find yourself in my shoes. It was a little over a year after Carmen passed away when I realized:

"My husband has a new wife!

I was shocked at first and contemplated how long it would last. She didn't take as long to get ready and she didn't laugh at the same jokes as I did. She didn't second-guess her words as much and she wasn't as afraid of change as I was. Her stride was different as was the shape of her hips. When I saw her, I wondered what my husband saw in her that made him stay.

Her eyes were more focused than mine. Her heart seemed both easy and impossible to break. It didn't seem like the weather fazed her and yet her plans were solely based on the amount of sunshine that day. She looked tired but tried to hide it. I could see through her and sometimes I saw myself in my husband's new wife.

I guess maybe that's why he picked her. She is quick to decide and slow to anger. She keeps the beat even when the music is off. She smiles more than she should and her hands fit perfectly in his.

Thankfully I have a new husband too!

His words are more carefully chosen. He walks both taller and steadier. My new husband understands silence and doesn't try to penetrate it. He is more decisive and has a calmer nature. He desires to lead, reassure, and love harder than my past husband. He is tired but doesn't like to show it.

He is gentle and inspires with just one glance at his new bride.
I know they will be together forever.

For it is not only the day that changes, but the people in the
midst of it. But change is not the enemy. Change is the
blessing. Change is the opportunity. Change is the only thing
we can count on. Change is the growth and change is
beautiful."

Dear bereaved couple,

I pray your heavy hands find one another. If not tonight, then soon.

I pray that extra breaths are taken when harmful words are about to emerge.

I pray you become surrounded by a community that lifts you up and allows you the space to reconnect over and over as you are transformed through your grief.

I pray for gentle reminders of your child to bring you together instead of tear you apart.

I pray that the waves of your individual sorrow can be seen clearly by each other and, with unmatched understanding, you can lift each other up over and over again knowing the fruit of your love will be the sweetest you've ever tasted.

Amen.

How Can I Help Someone Through Their Marital Battles?

We are the first to respond to the wedding invitations and we throw congratulatory posts all over social media like glitter, but when it comes to struggles within a marriage, society tells us to look away.

As a parent who has endured the last year and a half as a bereaved parent, I can confidently testify that the people who chose to build up my marriage, hold a special place in my heart.

If you care about someone who is grieving the loss of their child, please:

- Pray for the family as a unit.

- When you ask the mother how she is doing, do not forget to ask about the father.

- If you have the bandwidth, offer to take some of the stressors off of the parents. This can include cleaning, running errands, providing meals, and watching their other children. Financial gifts can allow breathing room for the grieving couple.

- While they may seem to be functioning fine, surround the couple in community. Do not disable the invites.

- There are many gifts available for grieving mothers, but a gift purposed for the father or parents combine, will be uniquely treasured.

Self Reflection

How has your spouse supported you most effectively since having lost your child?

What do you wish your spouse understood about your current battles?

How can you be more supportive to your spouse this week?

How could your friends and family assist you and your spouse this month?

Rebuilding My Army

As a new person who has been broken and reshaped by loss you are in need of soldiers that are equipped to wage in these battles alongside you. As you have most likely experienced, this is a difficult quest.

You may have had a group, a tribe even, prior to your trauma, that would be the first to lift you up. However, now they seem to fall short. You may have current friends, who you question their acceptance of your loss as reality, because they rarely mention it at all. And, bizarrely, there may be people to whom you never gave a second glance, that instinctively know exactly what you need.

"Why can't they see that my wounds are still bleeding?" She asked.

It was a serious question, one I had asked myself at least a dozen times, yet in that moment the answer became clear.

They *do* see. And that is what scares them away.

Bereavement can be treated like a contagious disease. I will be the first to admit that I am at fault for treating it as such.

I remember when Carmen was in the hospital, there were certain people who had lost children that kept loving on us throughout our dreadful day to day life. It always made my stomach churn. They represented something I never wanted to be part of.

Being the "mom of the daughter who died" is never how I wanted to be known. Yet, here I am, extending my heart, met with many who flee at the very thought.

Whether you've been met by the acquaintance who quickly changes the subject, the friend who has never brought *it* up, or the family member who hands out inspirational quotes like bandages, I am so sorry. Please do not be discouraged.

Hold tight.

Your army is being rebuilt.

"It was just after Christmas; the first without Carmen. I had been invited to a "slipper swap" with a bunch of moms. This may sound super fun and cute, but in that season of my life almost nothing haunted me more than surrounding myself with other moms.

Carmen had been in heaven for five months and I was newly pregnant with Mia. I was sick, achy, and still hadn't tested the social waters of my new life. And there would be moms there—lots of moms. It was a group that I should naturally fit in with and yet it was the group I dreaded entering. I had discounted the possibility of ever making a new friend after the death of my child. I assumed there was no way someone would want to stay after I lead with and unpacked that information.

On the way to the event, I pulled over three times. Twice I called my own mother for reassurance to keep driving. She told me 'Sydney, just try it. You don't have to stay long.' My anxiety was so heightened that I was gagging and sweating and even driving with my windows down in the middle of winter.

What would I have in common with these ladies? These are the ones who had just laid ground for their new pool while I laid my baby to rest and whose holiday hairdos looked like the top of a Christmas tree while mine had been confined to a bun for years. These are the ones who would complain of the cold when I was thankful for the excuse it gave me to stay indoors and hide.

I wasn't ready to meet new people. I hadn't even met myself yet.

I awkwardly entered the home and made sure to try and smile at everyone. Most of the women I had never seen before but it felt as if they had seen me. My heart pounded. I felt so alone.

Then, there she was—a stranger to me; cute, bubbly, and polite.

She leaned in close and whispered the words I had unknowingly prayed to hear.
'I know you and your story. I prayed for baby Carmen.'

The door was open. It was exactly what I needed. She didn't announce it to the world. She didn't fling herself on the ground and say she didn't know how I could do it. And she didn't keep her name to herself while staring at me from afar.

She said her name. It was all I needed. As the night continued this stranger cried tears of joy when she found out I was expecting. She referred to Holland as "big sister" and continued to use Carmen's name. It was as if she had been through some class titled "How to Interact Well with Grief-stricken Moms" and had passed with flying colors.

But God works in mysterious ways.

This stranger was not a stranger, but a neighbor. She lived right across the street from me and this stranger has become intimately involved in my day-to-day life.

She introduced me to the new mom that I am. She has given me confidence and pushed me out of my comfort zone. She has celebrated with me and given me permission to cry. She has cooked for me, loved on all my babies, and given me a new hope for the world and where I can belong.

Though she had not walked through those hospital days with me, attended Carmen's funeral, nor saw me hide for months, I now had a friend who was there waiting for me when the cards and flowers stopped coming.

Maybe I didn't think I was ready, but God had prepared her for me in my new battle as a bereaved mom. All I had to do was show up."

HOW CAN I HELP A BEREAVED PARENT BUILD THEIR ARMY?

This section of *Still Fighting* was the most difficult for me to formulate. During the creation of this book, three names were added to the dedication page. Three precious children with stories that impacted me personally were taken to heaven. Three exceptional families, left to continue their mission with massive holes in their hearts.

I should know how to help. I should understand this road and spill encouragement abundantly into their gaping holes.

I sat with my unfulfilled duties for quite some time and allowed myself to go back to the first day I became a bereaved parent. I peered into the memory of exhaustion and delusion accompanied by adrenalin that first week held. I pondered on laughing just hours after Carmen passed, not because I wanted to, but because I had to. I gave myself permission to witness what people around me did that kept me afloat, and I took note what was missing.

The first two weeks following Carmen's death, our home was a bustling tourist site. My husband is extremely extroverted and for him, comfort comes in the form of people. While I was genuinely appreciative of the family and friends that remained at my side, part of me knew that when they left, the real grieving would begin.

In many ways it was a blessing to have the people I care about most right next to me. They listened to my stories, planned the most incredible celebration of life service, fed me, and loved on Holland tenfold what I was capable of. But, I am a people pleaser, a planner, and a perfectionist. As much as I knew I didn't have to act a certain way, I seldom let my emotions take me to the place of sorrow I felt inside. I remained strong because it is a role that I have always gravitated to. Letting my tears flow could mean opening the flood gates and I had little energy to console others, even if it wasn't expected of me. The wear and tear that early grief exhorts is astounding. When caring for your bereaved friend, please take their personality into consideration.

In the early days, I wished that people had refrained from using past tense phrases. I was not in denial that Carmen had died, but hearing her name used with words like *was* or *had been* - stung. Even years later, it brings me joy when someone phrases their thoughts with compassion. For example, "Carmen is impacting my life because of her relentless fight."

Words will always lack, but truth spoken can be a solid foundation to hold on to. I craved for someone to remind me that I would always be Carmen's mother. It would have meant the world to me to hear that my role as her mom did not end because of Carmen's new location. This simple truth was something I played over and over in my mind and hearing it could have instilled powerful confidence in me.

Give space but do not give up. Reach out and do not be afraid of not receiving a response. For the hundreds of messages I received after Carmen's death, I mentally thanked each one. My fingers however could not form such simple sentences of gratitude.

Have *you* enlisted?

Whether you decide to fight in the foreground, the background, or beside your friend it is important to know that all positions are needed.

Know your strengths. Have confidence in your gifts, talents, and expertise.

If you are a cook, have you filled their home with delicious comforts even in the months and years following their passing?

If you are a listener, have you given up your time to hear their heartfelt stories? Have you called on birthdays, holidays, and any day that God has placed them or their child on your heart?

If you are near, have you made sure long periods of time do not pass without your presence in their life instilling confidence in your unwavering support?

If you are far, have you sent cards, letters, and gifts that have the ability to inspire your friend to hold on to a tangible token of love to prove their child has not been forgotten?
If you love them, have you joined them in spreading the love they carry?
And if you have absolutely no idea what to do, you have been given a special position.

You are in position to **ask**.

It is one thing that a bereaved parent will never tire of hearing, and one that is rarely spoken. What a joy it is when someone asks about our child or asks how we would prefer to be loved!

"How would you like to celebrate your daughter today?"

"Can you tell me about your daughter/son?"

"What would you like to do today?

Persist in loving your friend through this dark time.
Do not grow weary.

Say their name.

It's so easy. It's so simple. It's so powerful.

But many shy away.

For hundreds of reasons, when someone passes—especially a child—it becomes customary to not refer to them anymore.

If you know someone who is grieving and you don't know how to help, just say their name.

If it's been two days or two decades, say their name.

If it's their birthday or a random Wednesday, say their name.

If you were thinking of them for any reason at all, say their name.

If you're afraid the reminder will make them sad, put your feelings aside, and say their name.

It's the greatest gift you can give—the gift of remembrance, recognition, pride, care, and love.

Please just say their name.

Self Reflection

Who has been your greatest support after your loss?

Are there people in your life that may not fit well in your new army? Why do you feel this way?

How can you extend more grace to those that wish to love you through this time?

Freedom Song

I wonder when Jesus restored the blind man's sight, were people impressed by the miracle.

I wonder if the witnesses shrugged it off because we were created to have vision anyway. I wonder how long the man lived and what he did with his new sight.

I wonder these things because I began to put standards on God's miracles. I missed extravagant things because my timeline was different than that of the Lord. I missed beauty and excitement because I compared my miracles to those around me. I abandoned a deep, deep love because I could not see beyond my own two eyes at the miracles all around me.

To the baby who passed in his mother's heavy arms before she could whisper your name, you are a miracle. Your pure existence is the work of the Lord and your beauty and worth will never be forgotten. You were created by a loving father and placed on Earth for the precise time that your story needed to alter generations to come. You were loved before you were known and will continue to be loved for eternity.

You are a miracle.

Consumed by loss.

*We've lost moments, years and memories. We've lost
assurance, identity, peace of mind, and sleep.
We've lost the familiar—the "supposed to be" and our
"norm."
We've lost our way.
We've lost naivety.
We've lost our humor.
We've lost our title, our timeline, and maybe even our hope.*

*But from a great loss I have found a new song; a song of true
friends who do not judge or come with empty words but stand
firm inspiring and instilling in me a confidence to move again.
It's a song of compassion.*

*I found my drive. I found my oldest daughter yearning to
protect, understand, defend, and persevere. And I found myself
nurturing and developing skills I never prioritized.*

*When I lost her I found the intersection of my calling and my
action. I found out why the heartache of my past was God's
perfect plan. The passion of my heart suddenly had an outlet
that was needed and wanted.*

When I lost her I found my priorities. I found my voice.

*When I lost her I found my faith. Not faith in a "might be, a
maybe, a hopefully,"
but a faith that is firm and boiling over, genuine and selfless.
When I lost her I found my song of joy. Without shame, guilt,
or pressure I finally knew what it felt like to be happy since
happiness was now a choice and not merely a circumstance.*

When I lost her I found the woman I had always hoped to be—direct, unwavering, raw, bold, patient, curious, conquering, and tender.

When I lost her I found my song of freedom.
   Freedom to love hard.
   Freedom to smile whenever I wanted and cry equally as often.
   Freedom to stand up when my heart pounded and sit out when I needed rest.
   Freedom from the heaviness of this world.
   Freedom to view the sky as the window to heaven, and to have confidence in where she now resides.

When I think of the life ahead that I must endure without her I know she is always with me.

For in her loss beautiful ballads were orchestrated.

Forever changed.
Better.
Stronger.

She will remain on my breath and in my bones carrying me from day to day. Intertwined with my story we have become one.

Carmen,
If they hear my song, little one, they will hear you.

Beautiful.
Joyful.

Faithful.
Found.
Free.

You and I get to relish in the knowledge of the miraculous sight received because others were overwhelmed by one single moment and chose to share it with all existence.

Our children were miracles.
Miracles are never silent.
We are witnesses. Let us not keep quiet.

What will your song sound like?

Will your overabundance of love inspire you to become a generous giver? When your heart aches to reach up to heaven and dote on your angel, will you use your gift of compassion to become a blessing to others?

Will the melody created by the void you have be soft and tender, able to comfort others who can't see the next ten seconds of their life? Or will drums pound as you forge a new path of innovation and transformation? Will your trials set afire a testimony of grace and power because your child's life was more powerful than death?

Will you allow your song to alter the world as we know it?

You are the composer. You are the warrior. Their story will be your freedom song.

This battle is important and overflowing with grace. It is okay if you choose to fight for peace, truth or joy. It is okay if you are defending hope. With blooms in your left hand and a shield in your right, it's ok if all you do is fight. If your weapon of choice is a bold word or piercing silence, a sweet tune or an abundance of trumpets, it's okay if you're still fighting.

The war has already been won; the sweet victory of heaven awaits!

Self Reflection

How do you want to remember your child?

What is something you would like to do in honor of your child annually?

When your heart is ready, use the space provided to write a thank you letter to your child for the new song they have given you.

While in the dark she found a light...

...brighter than most will ever see.

Words from Warriors

Grief is unique to us each. Our stories may have the same ending, but our chapters are as rare and plentiful as the wildflowers. Understanding this truth, I sought out bereaved parents from across the country to spill their heart into this book. May you find comfort in this compilation and wisdom within their words from war.

"My son Landon taught me more lessons that I could count but one of my favorites was the redefinition of motherhood. We can't always see the scars and bruises that those around us carry. We don't know the road that got them to this point – so be gentle. Love fiercely. Live boldly. And never forget that there are hurting people, all around us, who just want to be seen. Regardless of whether you know he's there or not, Landon will always be a part of my life. A part of my parenting journey. Motherhood may not look like I'd imagined, but it's only *more* beautiful for having him a part of it."

"My son's stillbirth taught me of the fragility of life. There are no guarantees, no comfort in statistics or odds – simply Christ. And while that fact is sobering and at times disheartening, there is such great hope to be found. Astounding, unbelievable, grace-drenched hope. Walking through such loss has kept my eyes bound to an eternal perspective. It's brought heaven closer."

"We talk about him, visit his grave, and celebrate his precious life. Through these everyday interactions come incredible opportunities to discuss faith, eternity with Christ, and what it means to love someone who's no longer with us. While we keep the answers age appropriate, we never shy away from entering into and fully discussing the questions that arise. This is part of Landon's lasting testimony. We long for the day we will be reunited without our *whole* family, worshiping before the throne of God together."

"People always say loss parents are "brave" for going through what we've gone through. It's not true. We didn't have a choice. But what I think is *truly* brave, are those who choose to enter into the depths of our grief and love fiercely. It's not easy. Grief is messy. I'm not the same person I was before I lost my son, and that can make it difficult for others to reach out."

"Because of our family's loss history, my other son thought that all babies go directly from being inside a mommy's tummy to being with Jesus in Heaven."
…I told him that heaven was the best thing you could ever possibly imagine – and he promptly decided that meant his brother was swimming with Jesus in a big pool of cake."

-Liz Mannegren, author of *"Embrace: Clinging to Christ Through the Pain of Pregnancy Loss"* and bereaved mother of Landon Alarik Mannegren

"Even now, I feel pain and despair. How can I possibly do this for the rest of my time on this earth? Nobody understands the struggles my son, Bobby, was going through. I want to share ALL of his story but I don't feel I can be 100% honest about his life or death. When you loose a child to suicide, everyone assumes there had to be something the parents either did wrong or didn't do that they should have."

"We celebrate on February 11th every year because that is the day Bobby hung himself, the day my world was turned upside down. I plan a party to gather friends and celebrate Bobby. I surround myself by everyone I know… that distracts me from my pain. We have adopted a highway in his memory and our community comes together to care for it twice a year"

"When the guilt rises and the "why didn't I" screams, I quickly replace it with the truth that God numbered each of our days and knew exactly how Bobby's life would end. I quickly tell myself that all of the guilt and "what ifs" won't bring my son back so there is no purpose in it. It is the devil's attempt to take me down and by the power of the Holy Spirit I rebuke the lies. But my heart still breaks for my son, the pain he was in, the torment he lived with…"

"My son taught me that love always wins. He taught me to believe that people are hurting even if I don't understand. He taught me the destructive power of words. He taught me that sticks and stones can break your bones but words can kill. He taught me the mortal blow that Satan will take if you allow destructive words to play over in your head. He taught me that life is not fair but God is good. He taught me to be compassionate to LGBTQ people. He taught me that God will use ALL things for His glory. He taught me not to be afraid of

126

my own death but to look forward to it and rejoice in my heavenly, eternal home!"

"I went back to my work just six weeks after Bobby's death. I am a repertory therapist and I worked in the same unit that he passed away in. I took babies off life support and handed them to their parents to say their final goodbyes. I took final photos in the PICU and OR so mom & dad could have one last photo of them with their child. I sat with broken parents and shared what has helped me. I allowed myself time and time again to step into other's pain because I had been there and could stand side by side with them in their pain, in their grief, just so they would know they were not alone."

"Our family of five will never be together again until heaven. We remember the hole, the empty chair, the empty bed, the silent footsteps, the silent laughter. Every. Single. Minute. Of. Every. Single. Day."

"I attempt to forgive others up front for not knowing what to say or how to help or being caught up in their daily turmoil. I recognize that there is no way they can possibly understand what we are going through and that our pain consumes most of our day. They are able to forget that my son died but I am not."

- Nancy Collar, Respiratory therapist and bereaved mother of Bobby Collar

"Since my child was born still, I didn't necessarily have a chance to display love before he died. But the first time we visited his grave as a family of three (my husband and I along with our daughter), we left mementos on the headstone and my daughter wrote a love letter to the sibling she never met and left it at the grave."

"For a long time, I was weighed down by anger and jealousy. I can say that the feelings of envy still creep up when I receive a pregnancy announcement or see a pregnant woman or newborn."

"I've learned to treat people kindly. To listen more than talk. To understand that sometimes words that are meant to help, actually hurt and to use my mouth accordingly."

"I wish others could see that there is still someone missing. And that my subsequent baby did not replace the one who died. Even now, the presence of pregnant women and babies still stings. For the most part, I am happy for them now, but there is still hurt present. To those who want to help, please understand that grieving makes everyday tasks very difficult."

"Taking care of a living child, when I was dealing with the grief of losing one seemed impossible. One of my greatest fears is that while I was grieving, my living child felt unloved by me. I wasn't able to give the attention she needed and deserved and I fear she will carry that with her. Additionally, I fear that my children will die. I fear that having a still born baby is possibly preparing me for another loss in the future."

"I want my living children to know that God is still good and that their sibling is loved by Jesus just as we are."

"Those who have helped me most are honestly the people of the internet. I found some very supportive online communities for women who were grieving the loss of a baby. They seemed to be the only people who truly understand and who could truly relate to my pain."

"There are certain friends who slunk back after my loss. Who didn't offer to help. Who told me about all the women they knew who were pregnant, without seeming to understand it was a topic of conversation that was very painful for me. There are certain friends who simply didn't seem to acknowledge my grief."

"Sometimes words unintentionally hurt and just as I need grace during my time of grief, I need to extend grace to those who are trying to help, although imperfectly."

-Jenny Albers, bereaved mother of Micah Albers

"There is a constant weight of being incomplete. There is always a desire to shout to the world that I have given birth to three beautiful children. So much of me still needs the world to know."

"The Holiday season always feels pressure laden. How am I going to honor Keller this Christmas? How will I represent him in our Christmas cards? Should I save a seat for him at our Thanksgiving table? It all feels too much. It feels as though if I do not do enough, I don't love my boy enough. So often, I opt for nothing. I opt for thinking about him quietly in the corners as the kids open presents. His memory floods me as I fill my plate. I want to do more, but thus far, I've lacked the bravery to tackle something so large. How can anyone show all the love they have for a child who cannot be scooped up in their arms?"

"I'm never not thinking about him. Even now. Even 5 years later. Even today his presence in our daily routine and chaotic loved filled home was noticeably missing. I'm constantly imagining what our life would be like with a raucous, middle-child brother in the mix. I get mad that we don't have a van, because technically, we don't need a van. I am constantly comparing myself to mothers of 3, 4, 5 - I get mad because no matter what I do, I can't say I truly know what a life like that is like. I feel incomplete. Always. BUT. It's ok. I'd rather feel incomplete and still have my love for him intact."

"People don't know how to face tragedy and loss. It's not a class any of us ever took. (It should be.) Some people have a natural knack for coming alongside those in pain and being precisely what they need. Others - well - don't. I have found that most people do want the best for me. A lot however do not know how to offer up "the best". Gentle (or firm) guiding of what not to say to someone in grief is often needed. I remember looking squarely in the eyes of a dear friend who kept asking day after day if I was doing any better and saying, "I NEED you not to ask me that any more. I'm not doing better, and I won't be doing better for a very long time."

"I want to remember the day Keller was born forever. The day he was born was also the day he died. He emerged into and exited this world simultaneously. As counterintuitive as it sounds, I long to go back to that day. To live each moment over again. I want to feel the pain in order to feel Keller just one more time. But not just to feel Keller. The room God created in those 18 hours of labor was HOLY. I have never in my life experienced a more sacred space. The Holy Spirit filled the room almost tangibly. Each person who stepped into that room walked away forever changed. An amazing resident delivered our son. She was placed in the room by God. Another Doctor later shared that in her notes regarding the birth of Keller the resident wrote, "This will forever change the way I practice medicine." Amen. This will forever change...everything."

-Elizabeth Bartlett, bereaved mother of Keller Norman Bartlett

About the Author

Sydney Hatcher is a Northern Virginia native known for her unwavering smile.

In her youth Sydney used poetry to express herself. As a young mother, writing became a coping mechanism while she endured the rigors of extended hospital stays with her middle daughter, Carmen. The writing that grounded Sydney greatly impacted her community and led to the publishing of her first book, *Carmen "The PICU Baby"* in 2018.

With a heart for chocolate-covered pretzels and Jesus, Sydney seeks to live out her motto, "Every day is a good day." Alongside her husband, Nate, she has served as an international missionary and is blessed to have witnessed perspectives from 27 countries. She considers Pediatric Intensive Care Units as her new mission field and uses her gifts to encourage families of medically complex children. Sydney is the founder of Carmen's Miracle Makers Incorporated, a non-profit organization created in honor of her late daughter, Carmen Grace Hatcher.

For more information, please visit: www.CarmensMiracleMakers.org

A Note from Sydney

Dear Friend,

I am glad we have met, even if it is under these circumstances. I hope this book found you in a cozy corner where the light filled your room just enough to keep you leaning forward. I want you to know that however you feel right this moment, is more than okay. You are doing difficult things and you are doing them well.

If today is hard, which it rightfully may be, please know tomorrow will come. And if tomorrow comes and you laugh really loud, please understand that laughter is fine too. Your journey is not a manicured path lined with flowers, eloquently designed to keep you on the stepping stones. Your journey is a trail with rocks and sticks, large trees and boulders. You will have to crouch low and jump high to get to your destination.

But, my dear friend, I promise you, this trail holds pockets of perfection. There will be streams of peace and openings in the thick forests that are awaiting your arrival. The most beautiful sunset is being prepared with you in mind.

I would love to hear from you along the way. If this book comforted you, or if you gained the confidence to join someone else in their current battle because of these words, please let me know. You and I may have only met through paper, but forever you have a friend in me.

Love,

Sydney Hatcher

Follow **@StillFightingBattles** on Instagram
for continuous inspiration & updates on my next book!

Made in the USA
Middletown, DE
27 April 2020

90594158R00087